i

Biographies

Peter Martin was born in 1944 in Staffordshire. He
trained as a teacher, working in West Sussex, Suffolk
and at an adventure training centre in Scotland. When
a childhood passion for natural history re-emerged, he
embarked on a long career with environmental
organisations. He was the RSPB's Education Officer for
South East England, Head of Education for WWF-UK
and latterly Chief Officer for the South Downs Society.
He is now retired and lives with his wife in Seaford.

Previous poetry publications:
Seasons Regained, 2005
Ghost Music,   2010

Sarah Gregson grew up in Newhaven, and after
spending time studying and working in Bristol, London
and Paris, she settled back in Seaford with her three
children. Having worked as an illustrator and graphic
designer for many years, she started to paint when
caring full-time for her mother, who loved a good view
and passed that appreciation on to her daughter. The
paintings reflect the smallness of people against the
grandeur of the local landscape, and are inspired in
style by vintage railway posters; they accompany the
poems in remembrance of the artist's mother, Kay,
who died in 2012.

ACKNOWLEDGEMENTS

I am grateful to:

Patricia Martin for her critical first reading of the poems and her careful and sympathetic editing of the manuscript;

Tom Cunliffe for preparing a print-ready manuscript and for the cover design;

Joy Read for proof reading the manuscript.

Any mistakes that remain are all of my own making.

Kindred Spaces

Poetry of the Sussex Downs and Coast

Peter Martin

Illustrations: Sarah Gregson

Seacroft Arts

First published by Seacroft Arts in 2013
redfox.martin@btinternet.com

Printed and bound by
CPI Group (UK) Ltd, Croydon CR0 4YY

Text copyright Peter Martin
Illustrations copyright Sarah Gregson
Front cover and manuscript preparation Tom Cunliffe

ISBN 978-0-9564540-1-0

Front cover: Hope Gap, over the Seven Sisters to Birling Gap, Belle Tout
Lighthouse and Beachy Head.

Visit www.withaviewto.com or sarah@withaviewto.com for details of the
illustrator.

DEDICATION

To my wife, Patricia.

Contents

Kindred Spaces

Preface

Most of the poems in this collection and the illustrations that complement them, present 'portraits' of particular moments, at a particular time of year in a variety of places, each with its own unique human stories and environmental content.

This heady concoction of reality has an impact on all our senses, our emotions and imagination. So, from time to time, where we are changes from being a place we visit or pass through, into a space we engage with and for which we feel a deep affinity; these are our kindred spaces.

The poems and illustrations feature 'spaces' within six or so miles of the seaside town of Seaford in East Sussex. This is an area with stunning landscapes of chalk downs and sea cliffs, ancient villages and the largely undeveloped Cuckmere valley; it contains perhaps the most revered and emblematic scenery of the South Downs National Park.

The one poem from outside this area is 'Genesis at East Guldeford', set in the far east of the county; it features the 15th century parish church of St Mary's which has fine wall paintings of angels, dated around 1898, high above the altar.

All the poems were written between March 2010 and December 2012 and some relate to the following stories.

Washed Ashore: The English Channel has for centuries been busy with shipping. When wind and sails were the only means of propulsion, the dangerous and unpredictable currents around Beachy Head and frequent violent storms proved too much for many ships which were wrecked under the steep cliffs between Eastbourne and Seaford; subsequently, many bodies were washed ashore, many unidentified. In the 1700s, the Parson of Friston Church, Jonathan Derby, took it upon himself to have many of these unidentified bodies brought to Friston Church for burial.

His deep concern for shipwreck victims led him to take direct preventative action. He excavated 'Parson Derby's Hole' in one of the caverns in the cliffs near Beachy Head, where, during storms, he would spend nights setting and tending lights on ledges to warn passing ships of the dangers.

Devil's Door: These small doors are found in the north wall of some medieval and older churches. They originated at a time when ancient pagan beliefs lingered and mingled with Christianity. Early Christian churches were often built on sites of former pagan worship, the north side of the Church was considered to be the 'heathen' side and small doors were built in the north wall to allow heathen worshippers to enter. There was also a belief that the Devil resided in the unbaptised child's soul, it was driven out at baptism and the north door was opened to allow the Devil to leave. During the Renaissance and Reformation such practices were deemed irreligious and many of the doors were blocked up.

Tapsell's Gate: Churchyards were often gated to stop cattle and sheep from entering; however the standard five-barred gate is heavy and cumbersome. A Tapsell gate overcomes this problem by swinging on a central spindle, thus requiring half the radius of a five-barred gate for opening and closing; also, if well maintained, it will turn at the lightest of touches.

It is thought that these gates originated in Sussex, although there are only six examples remaining in the two counties. A number of Tapsell families appear in various parish registers in Sussex, but which of them was responsible for the design is unknown - although a John Tapsell lived in Battle in the mid 1700s and was a carpenter.

St Lewinna: Information about St Lewinna is scarce, and what is available is open to many interpretations and embellishment. What is clear is that she is the only recorded South Saxon Christian martyr and saint.

The South Saxon kingdom, modern-day Sussex, was the last of the Saxon kingdoms to convert to Christianity. This conversion was spearheaded by the exiled Bishop of York, Wilfrid, later St Wilfrid. He arrived in Sussex by boat at Selsey in 680 and made his missionary base there. It would seem that Lewinna was either one of Wilfrid's converts and became a missionary herself or she was converted later as the mission moved east. Sometime around 690 she was killed by a Saxon pagan, possibly by an axe blow to the skull and records say that she was 'buried at St Andrew's Church not far from Seaford'. The three churches with Saxon origins that fit the description are Jevington, Bishopstone and Alfriston. At some stage her relics were found to be capable of miraculous healing – a convenient attribute to convince pagans of the power of the new monotheistic faith of Christianity.

Jevington's claim to St Lewinna and her relics is based on the fact that a small priory was built in her honour. However, the fame of the miraculous bones spread and in 1058 two Belgian Monks landed at Cuckmere Haven, made their way inland, stole the relics and took them back to their own monastery in Flanders.

Sometime later the Jevington priory, by then an empty shrine, became disused, fell into ruin and the remains reused.

Church Tower: Quoins are cornerstones on buildings and lesenes are decorative pillars set into a wall or at the corner of a building.

As part of their steady invasion of southern Britain, the Romans created a port on a raised peninsular that was protected on three sides by a vast marshy tidal inlet - now the drained and farmed Pevensey Levels. They then built a road that led west to link this important beachhead to other parts of their expanding British empire. Around 290AD the port became a fort, Anderida, and was the main garrison post of this part of coastal Britain.

The remains of the fort can still be seen around the Norman-built Pevensey Castle.

West Gallery: As the name indicates, these were galleries built at the western end of Anglican and non-conformist churches. They were purpose-built for groups of instrumentalists that led choirs and congregations in the singing of hymns and psalms. This 'West Gallery Music' had its heyday from around 1740 to 1860. The instrumentalists were often those who provided the music for social events such as village dances, so that the range of instruments played and the standard of musicianship was extremely variable. The range of music they played could also be somewhat eccentric, including traditional hymn tunes, arrangements of the music of Handel and Haydn, or words and melodies composed by band members.

When pipe organs became more widespread in the smaller parish churches, the bands eventually became redundant; this change was actively encouraged by many of the clergy, either because they disliked the earthy nature of the music and singing or because band members often showed little respect for authority. The trend for pipe organs was also actively promoted by the Oxford Movement. This was made up of highly influential theologians and clerics, often associated with Oxford University, who wished to reinstate the traditions of theology, worship and ceremonies of high-church Anglicanism; it left no place for the home-spun, folk traditions of West Gallery music.

The Long Man: At 231 ft tall, the Long Man of Wilmington or Wilmington Giant dominates the steep scarp face of Windover Hill and is one of the largest representations of the human figure in the world. It shows what appears to be a man, holding a spear or a staff in each hand or possibly holding the edges of two open doors. The current, clear image appeared in 1874 when a shadowy outline, visible only in certain light conditions, was outlined in yellow bricks; these were later replaced with white bricks.

The first records of the Giant come from drawings made in the 18th century, the earliest in 1710; there are no known previous records in folklore, written histories, paintings or artifacts. However, the drawings indicate that the Giant appeared as an indistinct outline, and was therefore almost certainly created at a much earlier date and had become overgrown.

There are few firm clues to when it was created, who created it, what it actually represents and for what purpose, questions that have taxed archaeologists, historians and romantics for hundreds of years. Understandably, there are many different theories, at best based on circumstantial evidence.

Some suggest that monks at the nearby Wilmington Priory created it in the 14th century, either as an image of a pilgrim, or that their beliefs were more pagan than Christian and that it represents a pre-Christian God.

Others suggest that it is an heroic image or a boundary marker relating to a Saxon king such as Harold (C 1050), Alfred the Great (C 870) who had a palace nearby at Westdean, or Aelle (C 470), who led the Saxon invasion of southern Britain and fought a number of successful battles close by.

A Roman god or emperor are also suggested, however an excavation in 1969 uncovered what would appear to be the Giant's earliest outline in the solid chalk. Covering this was a layer of chalk rubble containing fragments that may well be Roman and thus would date the Giant well before the main Roman invasion of 43 BC. There is therefore the possibility that it relates to the settlement, ceremonial or burial earthworks on Windover and surrounding downland hilltops. If so, it would or could be of Neolithic origin, and thus be some 5000 years old, perhaps representing a Sun god opening the gates to let light into the world through which he then returns to darkness and the underworld.

Air Dancing: Queen of England, Children of Prosperina and Half Mourner are names that, in the past, have been given to three species of butterfly: dark-green fritillary, meadow brown and marbled white respectively.

The White Horse: Unlike the Long Man, this image, carved into the chalk high on the scarp slope of High and Over Hill and overlooking the Cuckmere river valley, has no ancient history and no myth or mystery. It is known that it was first cut in the 1830s, possibly to commemorate the coronation of Queen Victoria, and later, having become overgrown, re-cut in 1924 by two local residents to surprise their friends and neighbours.

From the slope of Seaford Head, looking across Hawk's Brow to the curved shingle beach of Seaford Bay, on to Newhaven Harbour and beyond.

9

Sea Watching

Waves mesmeric incursions
demand contemplation;
the inevitable regularity of
surge and turn, surge and turn,
a salutary reminder
of animate frailty.

Ethereal illuminants
lay pathways of sun-flakes,
tempting the ever hopeful
this way, that way
towards the enchantment
of Elysium.

North winds smooth surfaces
where cloud shadows darken
make believe islands;
there and nowhere,
eroded by the next
clearing gust.

Quicksilver marks the edge
with shift-shimmered thumbprints,
a guileless flirtation
of shall we, shan't we
keep the boundary
in permanent uncertainty.

Gulls in fidgeting flotillas
drift on undercurrents
until their urgencies re-engage;
we need to, we have to
cease procrastinating
before our purpose fails.

A disembodied trilling
alerts the core
to a wavering echelon,
onward, ever onward,
secure in the sun-haze's
dazzling veil.

Surge and turn, surge and turn
this way, that way,
there and nowhere,
shall we, shan't we?
we need to, we have to,
onward, ever onward.

Washed Ashore

The impact resonates,
innate contradictions reverberate;
fear of nature's raw aggression
delivering harsh taught lessons
on misplaced security,

or the heart flutter of earnings
to be gleaned at the tide's turning,
unless the scavenging scurf
teasing at the churning surf
picks the flotsam clean.

But then a sunless shadow's shock
draped between the glistening rocks
pecked, torn, dashed, and broken,
a sea-wrecked, rotted token
of sometime humanity;

an unkind, foetid obituary,
snagged by remnants of normality
but deserving some gesture,
a redemptive act to register
loyal kinship.

So defying further desecration
and purgatory's desolation,
snatched from nature's jealous maw,
strapped to planks with a sacking pall
and hauled up crumbling cliffs;

then through a valley's mocking dream
of meadow scent and woodland gleam,
of chestnut candles' un-flickering light,
of finches' reckless butterfly flight
and on to the church;

past the kissing gate's reminder
of joyful times when life was kinder,
to lay this anonymous form
among the named mourneds'
temporal immortality.

A wooden weather-beaten cross
is there to mark this poor man's loss,
and Washed Ashore are the words they chose
as the sum of what we need to know
of all our journeys.

Spring Singing

A once in a lifetime thing
is a blackthorn spring,
with wedding whiteness
in arcades of brightness
where nightingales sing.

A once in a lifetime thing
is a bluebell spring,
with bejewelling dewness
under fresh-leaved newness
where blackcaps sing.

A once in a lifetime thing
is a cherry tree spring,
where frail-flower neatness
spreads wind-blown sweetness
and chaffinches sing.

A once a lifetime thing
is every spring,
when a swallow's spriteness
sways the cowslips' slightness
and we all should sing.

Devil's Door

There is a certain logic to original sin
and a need to purge the devils within.
So at the earliest time,
with incantations at the carved font's edge
and the alchemy of blessed water, we pledge
new lives to God.

Torn from a warm and pliant soul
malign, mischievous and malevolent trolls
scatter in the flint clad chill;
like trapped wild birds they panic-flutter
seeking refuge from blessed words uttered
in this sanctified place.

The small door on the damp north side
gives safe passage to a place to hide
in nature's secular sanctuary.
So they bide their time, honing skills
in a domain immune to good and ill,
or right and wrong.

They shine the limbs of beech and ash,
gloss the buttercup's golden stash
and tip nettle hairs with poison;
they practice pride, they lie and boast
as they wait a new receptive host
to tempt and torture.

Such naive fervour to release these devils
into a world so prone to revel
in all they have to offer;
and as sure as night gives way to day
new disciples pass their way, succumb
and spread the word.

Offerings

In the valley they shear a nervous flock,
the bleating echoes around chalk bedrock,
and carried on a southerly blow
into mid-summer's transcendental flow,
joins the weft and warp of a tapestry story
woven in life-thread since before memory.
Crooning doves add love to the weave
and a phantom wren bequeaths joy,
baroque-bright from leaf-tangle dusk
where honeysuckle's early morning musk
fades in a June day's desiccating sun
that renders other singers dumb;
and all is subsumed in a temporal destiny
of creating today's offering to eternity.

From the top of South Hill, looking across Chyngton Farm to High and Over, flanking the gap where the Cuckmere river cuts through the South Downs.

Suspense

The year has sun-soared into summer,
the peak of the parabola is reached;
free of the spinning insistence of time
a weightless world waits on a painted canvas;
the stillness and silence are unnerving
as moments merge, reluctant to slip-slide
towards inevitable transformation.
In the suspended space, colourless
below a flamboyant feathering of cloud
but above subtle shaded galleries of green,
this neither earth nor heaven holds an animation
of flickering swallows and scything swifts,
which, in chasing cryptic purposes,
etch summer's requiem on a ripening sky.

Tapsell's Gate

Linking the memory of a village to the reality
of a church, a path skirts a wall
of rough-sculpted beauty, decorated
by nature's untutored artistic integrity
and animated by butterflies' preoccupied
dancing along webs of seductive scent.
Between secular industry and sacred tranquillity,
Tapsell's memorial swings its semi-circle
around a central spindle, renovated
when wood and metal succumb to antiquity.
No myth or miracles, no creed or credentials,
no passwords or piety for this inclusive gateway
that eases the way from cradle to the grave's finality;
a lasting homage to an enigmatic carpenter.

Saint Lewinna

Poor Lewinna, murdered for her mission
and pagan suspicion of another God;
made a saint for her misfortune and healing relics,
an honouring monastery built for pious clerics,
until thieving monks snatched the sacred bones
and sailed them to an alien home.
Her shrine, of miracle powers devoid,
was abandoned, plundered then destroyed.
But when sunset shapes the low hill's folds,
ancient stories are in outline told
as shadows on this sacrilegious field;
at night a mist-wraith laments and pleads
for remembrance in her neglectful home
lit by moonshine's mourning monochrome.

Artists and Lovers

There are artists' minds behind the refined
randomness of this modest arboretum:
a sculptor's hand in the juxtaposed shapes, lines
and textures of twig, branch, limb and trunk;
a painter's eye in the design and subtle shades
of flowers, foliage, seed and sepal;
a perfumer's nose in the sun-bathed
fragrance of needle, bark, and petal;
a composer's ear in the swaying harmonies
of a tree choir soothing an unruly wind,
and a harpist's imagined melodies
embedded in pale curves of soft timbers.
But there are lovers' hearts in the elation
of the lime flowers' all too brief intoxication.

West Gallery

The gallery should have been saved,
high on the wall at the western end,
where assorted villagers played
assorted winds and strings, depending on
who could scrape or blow through hymns
and keep the singers in tune and on the beat
by stamping and enthusiastic din.
But it was all too close to cottage and to street,
too close to village song and folkish dance,
too far from piety and esoteric mystery,
too far from ritual and sacred chants;
so the band was banished from parish history.
No need to turn to face the music now,
rustic quires have gone with the ox-led plough.

Saxon Carving

No-one is sure of its purpose or pedigree,
so all may contest the truth of this stony mystery.
Although there are some givens,
a thousand years old, that once lay hidden,
a man, it seems, sculpted in well-worn relief,
a bonneting halo, and depending on belief,
Jesus, St Michael, St George or a pilgrim;
a pose as though at an artist's whim,
one hand on hip, a trophy stance, the other
holding a staff, a cross, sword or lance
thrust into a dragon's or Satan's puny maw.
But the beast is a meagre icon for
the dark-dream fear of a devilish hell
which requires the saints or God to quell.

Church Tower

Ties and frameworks of quoins and lesenes,
red bricks from the road to Anderida
and dark mirrors of flint create the essence.
And its purpose? A sanctuary in times of fear,
a stability for bells to warn, invite or celebrate,
and sacred protection for smuggler's gain.
A four-square landmark, decorated
by a golden cockerel above a weather vane,
reminders of betrayal and the wind's
significance in predicting an arrow's flight,
or if the weather would be mean or kind;
a collected history of the village's life,
that in its damp-chill heart stumbles and stalls
among dust-clung chairs and flaking walls.

Churchyard Yew

So much competition to claim my purpose and heritage
and thus justify my imposing, ancient presence.
A pagan icon warding off evil spirits, a purifier to assuage
the putrefying essence rising from insecure graves;
a Christian symbol of life everlasting and resurrection,
or a handy source of wood for English bowmen
seeking refuge, respite and divine protection
within the nearby, thick-walled sanctum.

God's design or Nature's chance give dark perenniality,
poisonous leaves, sickly red fruit with a lethal dart,
the bruised lividness of limbs contorted by longevity,
spiders and bats secreted in my hollowing heart;
these are the stigmata that are guilty of encouraging
this contradictory junk of perverse memorabilia,
this myth and fantasy that subvert my simple being
with witchcraft, allegory and necrophilia.

How I covet the translucent leaf bursting of spring
and the glister of autumn's fireglow splendour.
Sixteen hundred years is too long for lingering envy,
too long to be a silent witness to human endeavour,
to be tortured by ever-repeated mistakes and pain;
too long an emblem kept upright by struts and chains
that bite when gales tug and flail. I crave release
so I might die gracefully and find my peace.

From the slopes of South Hill looking up the valley of the Cuckmere river winding its way from the distant Weald, past Windover Hill and Exceat then on to the sea.

Sloe Gin

The pleasure is not merely
in the kick of garnet-glowing liquor
or the metamorphosis of astringent fruit;
there are a year's memories in the flavoured
harmonies of this infusion.

It all starts in the fragile cusp
when winter and spring vie for the season
and I sense the significance of the hedgerow's
bold whitening, a relict anticipation of
beneficence within such blossoming.

This vernal surge stirs an unreasoned
desire to seek out the phantom incense,
and risking the intimacy of thorn-ringed stars,
lose my heart to the fragile elegance
of sun-drawn sweetness,

witnessed by a peregrine on the wind,
hitting an updraft from the sycamore copse,
hanging on threads of exhilaration
and with a mere flicker and tilt
spreading trepidation across the valley floor.

Later, after the inevitable
fickleness of a blackthorn spring,
the effusive musk of hawthorn beguiles,
bird choruses sing the day in
and their vespers reconcile light to darkness.

The time is then right to follow sheep tracks
circling encrusted, sculpted bushes, leaning
into the contours of a steep down slope,
and there, pay my respects to green-set fruit
hoping for exclusive treasure.

Soon follows the many-coloured times,
the marguerite, bedstraw and thistle time,
the marbled, bronze and sky-blue butterfly time
and that magic time when all combine
in the refined nightglow of summer.

This kaleidoscope enriches the ripening,
until the near-distant sea that draws
a pastel palette from the sky's bequest,
is framed in red festoons of haws
and the full, black sloes are set for harvest.

So I bear the scratch and piercings
from thorns masked by elfin antlers
and pixie cups of hoary lichen;
a penitential bleeding for stealing
this essence of the seasons.

St Martin's Butterfly

The last day of St Martin's little summer
is a specious valediction of brightness
that leaves rain-flattened grasses,
wind-cropped contortions of elders
and spent heads of thistles un-resurrected.
Tempted from the safety of ivy's evergreen refuge
by this late sun's treacherous seduction,
a dried-leaf fluttering of black, red and white
seeks nurture from a barren landscape
closed down to face imminent winter.

There is no way back from this dream-wish
of a time of fragrant flowering and loyal sun;
the colours too faded, the frailness too advanced,
the desiccation beyond any redemptive offering
of honey on dampened fingers.
The cycle of seasons has worn the fabric thin
and the heart grows old and aches.
So collect windfall apples, bring in wood,
light the oven and scent the air with cinnamon,
cloves and nutmeg and revive the spirits.

Winter Barbeque

November the twenty first was no date
for a beach barbecue; cold from a northerly blow,
the sea a steely sheet, no silver plate
or reflected glow. In the all-absorbing grey,
gulls and crows relinquished their polarised colour,
pebbles held an uncharitable latent frost,
even the cliffs seemed diminished, their pallor
sullied and their summer drama lost.

Five women in headscarves, we did not intrude,
some young children, one in a red velvet dress,
the only colour in this brooding afternoon;
set in a recess below the ridge of the beach's
shelving edge, a tableau of refuge from the wind
and out of reach of unsympathetic eyes.
In the centre of their circle, a shallow pan,
we imagined spiced lamb, vegetables and rice.

The chill subdued any tang of cumin or cayenne,
but an air of contentment warmed the mind
and thawed the senses. Maybe this haven on a bay
of inclement weather and little winter charm
is better than they might have left behind.
We waved an apology for our inquisitive gaze,
the least we could do to repay their kindness
for sharing the enjoyment of this unlikely day.

Sea Smoke

Along the path skirting the top
of the dry valley, fresh snow was marked
by latticed tracks of predator and prey,
indicating no coincidence,
only a record of diligent searching.

A wind-drifted sea-smoke pulsed brightness
across an undulating fantasy of snow blossom,
making mountains out of modest hills
and spirits on numinous cloudscapes
out of the unworthy.

Other familiarities were reformed,
appearing and disappearing
as ephemeral amalgams of elements,
only the river and fresh-washed beach
were free of the snow-mist's alchemy;

crows and winter-grey wading birds
foraged among sea-shone stones,
gulls patrolled coldly lethargic waves,
and somewhere on the camouflaging shore
a curlew called an unconvincing defiance.

Verdigris-black and starkly white against
the enhanced grandeur of cliffs,
a ragged flock of lapwings seeking
salvation in an icy wilderness,
etched lost-soul tragedy on frozen air.

Janus

January sun loosens winter's tenacity,
interrupts its moving and shaping,
easing its disregard for suffering;
there are soft-voiced harmonies
as hopers and dreamers breathe deeply.

January sun silvers sculpted curves
and highlights low-tide banks,
where storm-ripped reed stalks
and flood-warped fence lines
create an unkempt artistry.

January sun sparkles the spray
as gulls bathe in sky-lit pools,
oystercatchers and shelduck
mirror their pied extravagance
while cloak-hunched herons bask.

January sun draws out a lark's
tentative cadenza and downland stirs;
woodland dankness absorbs
a robin's unpolished aria
and bare-branch buds revive.

January sun purples beeches
sloped on the valley's containing hills,
while on flood-sodden meadows
winter geese graze the greening
in this ambiguous brightness.

Looking east from High and Over across the Cuckmere valley to Charleston Manor, dating from the early years of the Norman Conquest, and beyond to Friston Forest.

Winter Geese

White-fronted for the specifically minded,
Anser albifrons for those who favour
the pretention of exclusive knowledge;
they fly tight-flocked on grey-patterned wings,
yelping in communal excitement or anxiety
and circling as if unsure of the compulsion
to retrace their snow-driven journey,
and chase receding ice towards unsetting suns.

Serpentine relics of salt-marsh creeks
create a stage for this valedictory scene,
with a backcloth of sheep-dotted downs
leading to a bastion of cliffs; and the story?
A mystery of a king's palace and his battle fleet,
the tragedy of a lost village, ghosts of smugglers,
the romance of a winter's brief infatuation,
and the emptiness when dreaming ends.

The Long Man

A track leads across chalk-stone fields,
others, left and right along the far margins,
converge under the upturned keel of the downs;
each is sparse with the comings and goings
of singletons, couples, families, slipping
and sliding on winter-spread mud,
except where rain in leeching rivulets
has sifted soil from its shingle bed.

At the intersection, for some an objective
for others a crux of diverging strands,
most hesitate, some pensive, reflecting
on a giant in outline guarding marchlands
between the clarity of ripple-shadow waves,
wind-driven across neat-rowed greenness,
and the ridge with mounds of ancient graves
made mystic by brightness beyond the rim.

So little is known, but so much admired,
so many enigmas, but so many notions,
so much sought and so much desired
from a figure that shuns both fact and fiction.
You may have never walked these tracks,
but you will know the whys and wherefores,
deep within the double helix and etched
into all our unremembered histories.

Sometime you will have sought his protection
from invisible pulses that thrash and moan
among the decayed dejection of witch-grove trees,
where devil-birds rise with spite-thrown curses.
Sometime you will have sought his wisdom
to find your place in the seasons' endless gyres,
or give answers to the hurtful beauty of suns
that set in billows of self-consuming fires.

Sometime you will have needed belief
that he would open the gates for beloved souls,
easing the grief of their final journey;
sometime to be a vast, consoling god,
confirming we are more than lonely stragglers,
staggering along uneven track-ways
and worth more than all our puny weakness.
And I need him today.

Snowdrops

A flower of an uncontrived calendar
that heralds a frost-purged, rain-washed,
colour-drained, wind-whipped,
reluctant ending of nature's cycle.
Spring, summer, autumn, winter,
a more satisfying ordering of the year.

This 'Timely Flowered Bulbous Violet',
lovingly planted to remind the faithful
of a virgin's purity, is a mutable symbol
now flourishing with profane meanings
in ancient churchyards, ruined monasteries
and bygone village hedges.

A lost sacredness, but a joyful integrity
celebrating the cusp with a certainty
that, as its Candlemas purity sullies,
tenor and treble bleating will underscore
a chaffinch's blossom-song, and day-by-day
the new year will be coloured in.

Dog Violets

The earth and sea are pastel-pale with chalk
and winter-shaven turf wide-eyed with violets,
delicate among the coarseness of desiccated stalks,
but bold enough to engage preoccupied minds.
The air is warm enough to free gorse's gilded musk
and choreograph sprite-gnats' mesmeric choirs,
the breeze enough to trouble the flower-heads' trust
and impede a red-tailed bee's clumsy desire.
Earthly larks, earth-coloured, crouch to hide among
tangled grass and stunted briar, their music bound
by uncertainty, not sure that the untried voice
will release the notes to sound and soar,
extolling the cascading joy of unkempt places,
of lambent skies and unnamed spaces of the heart.

Valentine's Day

I say I love you every day,
like how are you, good morning,
what a lovely, stormy or merely grey,
delete as appropriate, dawning.
So is the greeting commonplace,
just dutiful words that impart
little trace of thought or substance?
Or does it stem from a lens within the heart
that can reform a rainbow's gleaming
and give life's scattered colours meaning?

From Haven Brow, the most westerly end of the Seven Sisters cliffs, looking across Cuckmere Haven to the coastguard cottages and Seaford Head.

Cliff Fall

The picture in the loft has not aged, except the frame
has lost some gilding and dust has gathered on the glass.
To the uncritical eye, the scene is much the same as
when some thirty years past, the artist sat sketching
the promontory's curve, gorse, deep rooted in solid turf
and a fulmar's planing flight above a low tide.
But the gorse is diminished, clinging to crumbling earth,
the headland is less, jackdaws jostle and jibe
in wind-tousled feuds over cliff-face holes
and gulls cast shadows across widened shoals.

Eroding rain, the driven wedge of freeze and thaw
and desiccating sun have split the ground,
then vandal waves have tumbled bedrock to the shore.
There is indulgence in the profound sadness
of losing the last blossom-days of spring,
but when assumed permanence fails,
as cycles end that have no new beginnings,
then sorrow that cannot be salved prevails.
As the unambiguous edge creeps ever nearer
the inconceivable becomes clearer and clearer.

Genesis at East Guldeford

Named after the man whose family was named
after the ford where marigolds grew.
But here, where the land was claimed from the sea,
ditches are strewn with reed and yellow iris,
and where sheep safely grazed he built his church.
A simple barn with no gargoyles, ornate tracery,
triumphal tombs or carved capitals perched
on elegant columns. But there are angels in this place
telling the story of this small corner of creation.
They are not swan-winged, robed in scintillations,

these angels are coy, eyes demurely cast down,
dressed in homespun cloth the colours of nature,
their halos subdued like driftwood crowns
and above the clouds, hover on wings of folded paper.
Of their number, four form a modest band
of cymbals, cornett, psaltery and plucked rebec;
two more carry censers with flowery garlands
to sweeten the smell of toil with stock, plough or nets,
and six carry wreaths that frame a half-seen tale
of pastel normality that celebrates the mundane.

The first day is a storm, driven over turbulent waves
from whence, on the second, flat pastures rose;
on the third day oaken forests enslave the Weald
where timber for the church beams was chosen;

on the fourth, moon and stars fill the hemisphere
to guide the night fleet; on the fifth, white birds bring
life to open skies; on the sixth, man and women appear
and despite callow nakedness given dominion over
all things.

The blood and sap of all that had been created ran cold
and the pulse of the earth trembled with foreboding.

Air Dancing

Halfway up this monumental headland
a seductive plateau invites judicious resting
before the steep-slope testing, catching breath
while contemplating a gull-flight panorama
of drift-curved coast and a town folded in summer.
But stray from the engraved path to Hawk's Brow
and an obscuring brightness endows
each wayward step with anxious excitement.

Lured by the challenge of the void,
sidle towards the uncompromising divide
where a vertiginous drop meets a curdling tide
and crystalline waves scatter star-spangles
that confuse the eyes and daze the mind.
The body sways in the threshold's thrall
and appalling whispering commends
air-dancing to oblivion, spiralling

down through a sickly stench
of sun-rot sea-weed and fish-gut bird lime
that cloaks the descent past serpentine
guardians perched on knife-edged plinths
and chuckling demons in vertical labyrinths.
Step back, free of dark-dream fantasies
and fill the head with sweeter reveries
induced by the alchemy of the sun.

Drugged by perfume dispensed on the breeze,
lulled by crickets and grasses' restful rhymes,
recline on bedstraw, Spanish root and thyme;
then, soothed by gulls' down be beguiled
by cushions of ermine and purple crowns,
where the Queen of England's gilded grace,
Children of Prosperina, and Half-mourners enlace
a season's essence into butterfly lives.

Slack-tide Summer

There is compulsion
in a sea-wind that billows tree sails
and moves the day forward,
causing lambs to bewail its momentum.
But in the shelter of the scarp, summer
wallows in a season's slack tide,
lulled by a soundtrack of almost
silence, disturbed by a hush of leaves,
a scrap of wren-song from the hawthorn
and a blackbird's recap of spring.

There is an insistence
to cross the lichened stile
and take the track that curves
towards cut-corn gleam, but a desire
to stop and dream by a wayfarer tree,
its way-marker whiteness ripened to redness,
and lie in filigree grass where scabious,
agrimony and rampion attract other seekers;
then, in suspended no-when time become
enfolded in myths of immortality.

Short Days

There is little joy in ochreous leaves,
dried out, clinging to a woodland's lee,
a token resistance on winter's eve
that give no substance to the fingered filigree.
There is little warmth in the sun's low scan,
a pale and fitful sham that skirts the rim,
hurries the day through its colourless span
and un-tempers the chill of an unhindered wind.
There is little hope in the fallow fields
empty of the thrill of scintillant singing,
devoid of stirring wing-dance reels
and unperfumed by mosaics of blossoming;
only cruciform crows in unruly flight
croak distain at the dimming of the light.

Winter Heliotrope

They thrive on the edge of unlikely places,
the unloved, looked-over and left-over spaces,
where the mower never reaches and soil is thin,
where one thing ends and others are yet to begin.
Only those who kneel, as in self-conscious prayer,
lift the unlovely flower, and care enough
to breath the almond air, know that sometime soon,
when stems are flattened by winter's rime
and the final petals of previous summer fall,
when all seems dead and the year has stalled,
these defiant buds in shabby corners survive,
and come the thaw their crystallised scent revives.
Flowers of the sun when there is no sun
reassure that in the darkest days, hope lives on.

Down Town

Herring gulls wail, whinge and whicker
from their roof top and sky-scape homes,
disturbed by a hawk or internecine bickering
as this year's tiresome young are disowned.
Hysteria has spread and jackdaws chase,
chack and chow past chimneys and aerials
while starlings in shape-shifting races
entertain urbanity with ephemeral art.
The gulls quieten into petulant calm,
down feathers snow-flake onto the street,
jackdaws revert to inquisitive charm
and starlings settle on their church-roof retreat,
wheezing and whistling their vesper hymns
as a belated sun sinks and the light dims.

New Moon

The wind has dropped to nothing,
only the soul is stirring;
the sun has sunk into a disquieted sea
leaving translucent bands
of the unnamed colours between a rainbow's strands;
no vibrant flames of red and orange,
only a visceral burning.
There is a hint of frost that sharpens thoughts
of tomorrow, while winter gnats dance madcap jigs
under an evening star that skirts the dark-down
and flirts with filigrees of poplar.
In the space between reason and irrational sorrow,
crows chime the hour that heralds night-time's mystic arc
and blackbirds proclaim distrust of the gathering gloom.
As colours fade, a ghost of fullness
is clasped to a sliver of moon, an omen of brightness
that, sometime soon, will defy the dark.

Midwinter

Midwinter's solstice is past,
though nothing marked the turning point,
light-time spurned the moment
and dark-time's deepness lasts;
even a waning moon's wan cloud-glow
has gone, leaving the sky to constellations,
their scintillations as unilluminating
as the horoscopes that fancy bestows.
Before the sadness of half-light takes hold
and transforming night-chill bites,
a robin sings a solitary song that ghosts
from the darkest shadows, a bold soliloquy
that in its hopefulness, rebukes the folly
of self-indulgent melancholy.

Almanac

There are dates already marked in diaries,
deck the halls, paint eggs, change the time of dawn,
and others transferred each year, for fear of forgetting,
send a card, buy flowers, uncork wine and raise a glass.

But there is no space for ephemeral anniversaries
that ghost from the crowded almanac of the mind,
when the conjunction of season and chance encounters
evokes a kaleidoscope of reminiscences.

A red fox running becomes a sun-shone shape
leaping the brook of yesterday's clouds,
and the first brimstone of spring an errant planet
crossing a fallen-sky of bluebells;

sallow catkins' immoderate springtime yellowing
becomes snakes, damp from winter chilled water,
that twined fingers for warmth, while
wide-eyed peacocks sipped reviving nectar;

a froth of elderflowers becomes the pastel day,
all straw hats and lady's lace, when we stole
sweet-cream scent to ferment and, come the winter,
drink the essence of summer;

a flurry of reed-mace down becomes swallows
that chaffed and chased a threatening hawk
above the ecclesiastical purple of orchids
and powder-blue of forget-me-nots.

The scent of bedstraw, gorse, estuaries at low tide,
a rainbow mellowing a dark sky above delinquent waves,
the magic wand of wood-smoke, the fluting of a woodlark,
and a thousand other cherished moments waiting.

Birdwatching

High and over High and Over two buzzards inscribe
dark lines against a benign backdrop that belies
the crunch of frosted mud and ice-dull fingers of ditches.
Even higher, above where a lattice of snow lingers
on furrowed fields, gulls engage in magic tricks,
wide-wheeling against a white and blue fabric of sky,
into the sun and out, I may be gone, I might remain.
Below, on the valley's slope, grimy ewes, fleeces stained
by weather and birth-blood shield the first-born
against shadows that haunt winter-worn fields.

Between downland spurs that flank where the river
from a grey-hidden Weald slithers against
a filling tide, a peregrine heads towards the Haven,
untroubled by a small hawk's harassing; even a raven's
high dark crucifix fails to hinder the falcon's steely flight
towards the sculpted white of seven bright siblings.
Keening gulls proclaim the prodigal's return
to a refuge of whipping winds, of churning waves
and crumbling rocks on a sheer cliff-face,
a place of uncertainty that instils no trace of fear.

On firmer ground where turf has flattened
into an ochreous memory of scented patterns,
five plovers, all gold spangles and perturbed anxiety,
pipe a tune in a minor key with wandering words,
going anywhere, going nowhere, seeking a haven
until the thaw comes and steels the craven heart.
When their eyes are clear of mists of exile sadness
and the spell of hapless forgetfulness is broken,
then the sky will fill with well-known symbols
and their hearts with music from hymnals of home.

From Downland footpaths above Litlington looking
towards the White Horse carved into the steep slopes of
High and Over.

On The Ridge

Today is a squinting brightness day,
a sway to the metronome of walking day,
a warmth-drugged introspective day
until a rain-ridged path and widening horizons
interrupt brooding meditation.

From a bird's-eye vantage
only the frame, square-on, is a detail of senses;
to the left and right, genesis and destiny
are misted memory and sun-dazzled conjecture;
the centre is sufficient.

Within this crucible of vision and imagination
there is a breathless day, a no hurry
to do anything day, a no need to burst
into febrile springtime just yet day; although
two chaffinches trade tunes in the blackthorn.

Below, widgeon whistle from remnant pools,
rooks confer, neatly candled around ash trees
and, swirling down the curling river's valley,
unchoreographed gulls litter paper trails
against a dustiness of forest trees.

Closer, between desiccated stems,
a butterfly flaunts surprising brightness,
even though it is a nectarless day, a too soon
for brave gestures day, a much too soon
to celebrate surviving winter's day.

But streaming from the glint and glister,
celestial gossamer tugs the tilting,
turning earth towards another season;
this uncertain stillness will pass
as yet more days slough off into mist.

Planetary Conjunctions

Between the ides and the equinox
lambs bleat from silhouette hills
where a breeze blows evening chill,
gathering no scent from trackside thorns.
Closer, anonymous birds in muted singing
herald an afterglow of vivid stains,
which, before it fades proclaims
a trick of perspective and wishful thinking;
for Venus's love, born of sea-foam
outshines Jupiter's warlike thunder
and rekindles years of eroded wonder
at the myth-gods' scintillant home.
So revel in the brightness of their symbolic affinity
and drink a valedictory toast to preoccupations,
prosaic illuminations and second-hand sensations
of a bricks and mortar reality.

The Cuckmere Horse

Yesterday's omens brought high expectations;
a swallow, wings coloured by exotic sun,
violets' mosaics of lazulite fragmentations,
and cuckoo flowers' fragile colouration
of coarse relics of best-forgotten years.
Today's are ambivalent; an echoing incantation
of eponymous notes sung to a grey sky,
and blackthorn's off-white illumination
of tarnished sallows and frayed, faded reeds.

So we look to the graven image for inspiration
drawn from a time of heightened sensations,
when eloquent meanings and telling implications
imbued the earth and sky, and when horse,
boar and bear were worthy of veneration.
But there is no magic in this shallow indentation,
fashioned with care, high on the steep scarp slope;
simply a landmark cut into soiled chalk
and challenged by nature's unimpressed desecration.

Spring Storm

Yesterday the wind backed to the south,
not a capricious breeze but a rolling roar
urging banks of white-crest breakers
with dull drum-thud reverberations against
a shuddering beach, where spume and squall spat
and sprayed shrouds into the grey gale, to soak
and salt the bowed and battered hinterland.

Only the ocean's acolytes rode the storm,
gannets' bright crosses, skuas' piratical antithesis,
gulls and petrels, grey as mariner's fantasies,
revelled in the exhilaration of their birthright,
playing on the gust and swell, the troughs and peaks,
swaying and sweeping on a stage of wild waves
to the percussive beat and moan of atonal choruses.

Last night the storm abated and an untidy sea
regained a stained equanimity. On the tide line
gulls joust over jetsam, and seafarer-dressed,
a beachcomber collects clean washed cuttlebones
destined for exotic captives, with only relict dreams
of wing-lifting winds, of streaming rain,
of louring clouds and unframed horizons.

May Day

A kestrel observes, feathering the wind shifts,
drops, hesitates, seeking focus within confusion;
a blackbird listens, intense as his music and sifts
significance from a soundscape of sensations.
A swallow dips over a winter-filled dewpond,
then slips through warming air on spun silk wings
towards the rightness of destinations beyond
a whitethroat's paean to the sunglow of spring.
In this mosaic of subconscious harmony
a rambler ignores the bizarre insignificance
of spider orchids, cowslips' seasonal testimony
and black gnats' drunken dance over umbels of scent.
On this May day a spectral moon hangs in judgement
on which of these is deserving and which has lost its way.

On Common Ground

Hedge parsley lines the lane with lace,
elms, green-leaf the containing greyness,
horse chestnuts' kindled candles splutter
and swallows' stuttering season-chivvying
is gusted away on wave-mists of rain
that modulate the crowing of a vain cockerel.

But the village wears the day with comfort,
riding the rhombus round and round the pivot
of its church, as it was, as it is, a fine but modest
monument to a shadow time of scratched dials,
of unsaved memories and cryptic histories
engraved by arrow-heads on porch-side stones.

Inside the boundary walls, cowslips
bring a rejoicing of the little hills to the doors
and into a chilly sanctuary where plain glass
welcomes brightness; when night comes to pass,
sixty hanging candles lighten the darkness
and heighten the aura of immutable sanctity.

For a joyful sound an organ adds flutes and strings
to the comforting words of psalms and hymns
that enrich this simple space, where no marble effigies
flatter the wealthy, no coloured images honour the
saintly,
only an angel of clay giving an earthly benediction
to those who care to pray on this common ground.

Silhouettes Across the Sun

Hawthorn brightly lights and sweet-savoury scents
a sun-baked track of sculpted chalk, clay and flints,
a fabrication of accidental art and foot-trodden histories.
And all is as it should be, as a chaffinch sings of childhood
and a greenfinch ease-eases the day into meditation.
Blackthorn is spent and elder buds are ready to break;
soon, too soon a thrush laments from the ghosted grove,
remember, remember and sigh when we reach the gate;
not the makeshift rusted gate, secured with faded twine
and decorated with wind-woven and iron-dyed wool,
but the wooden gate that opens too easily, too urgently,
the wooden gate where hedge parsley's fragrant filigree
masks a pungent ditch and bramble tangled barbed wire.
There is no way to left or right nor any time for waiting,
only the path past where badgers sleep away the day,
then on to the edge where ravens track silhouettes across
the sun.

Elf Sickness

Enchanter's nightshade enchants the corners
of an unenchanting wood, where wind-shifting,
leaf-flickering mosaics of light fail to illuminate
false scorpions and poison fanged centipedes
that feel their way through unknowable realities,
untroubled by a vandal wind that scatters the scent
and browned leaves of an unfulfilled season,
unmoved by disembodied midsummer music
that attempts a fitful therapy from the canopy;
leaving the miniature perfection of subtle flowers,
white glisters sparking from a lucifer wand,
to cure the malevolent contagion of elf-sickness
that inhabits the secret darkness of the forest floor
and invades the vulnerable spaces in the mind.

Farmyard

It is a place between a starting point
and a destination, functional, unexceptional,
ignorable, with no pretence of aesthetic merit,
although in corrugated barns spring is heralded
with the birth of lambs that are soon marked
with blue graffiti and sent to frolic in the fields,
the season's saccharine symbols freed for fattening.
Later, muck and mud on the trampled track support
swallows' purposes, and when the wheat is cut,
stored straw brings the scent of ripened fields,
neat rolled and plastic wrapped. Come winter,
wind clatters loose panels, rain rattles roofs,
soiled cattle bellow and steam in foetid shelter
and a monochrome dankness unifies elements.
Beyond the yard, broken walls, rust-red gates
with make-shift fastenings of twine and wire,
merge with ragwort, mallow, nettle and hogweed
in summertime's attempt at untidy restoration;
further still, nature's progressive domination
brings a gentle transition to places beyond
music without melody, fact with no fantasy,
art with no artifice and rhythms with no rhyme.

From the Downs above Bishopstone, looking across the village with perhaps the oldest Saxon church in Sussex and towards Seaford Head in the distance.

74

Conversations

On the lichened porch a makeshift gnomon,
moves ancient hours as unnumbered shadows;
among faded marguerites and budding bedstraw
forget-me-nots plead for the forgotten, and yarrow
divines unwritten histories for those who care to dream,
half hidden by seeding grass, bryony and mallow,
and watch the path from the lychgate for the ones
who come to share the bench and their sorrows.
'If you don't mind, it's my old legs, wear and weather,
and lonely without my wife, with no-one to follow
the geese,
pen the ducks and hens, cook pigeon at the hearth,
and tend our little patch of cotters earth.

Not my poor daughter, she was sick and died;
she loved to hear thrushes sing from the copse
by the river where we netted fish on incoming tides,
or walk to the mill on the Downs, to collect flour,
make cheese or watch the thatcher tend his hives.
But oh the harvest home, with cider from the press-
house,
a roast pig, with bread from the bake house on the side;
go fetch the fiddle player, or sing me a verse
about the shepherd, his ewes, dancing lambs beside
the hogs, rams and fat wethers that made a fine show,
and remember the men from the wooded Weald
who sheared sheep, penned with hurdles in the fields.

My son was a shepherd boy, on the downs night and day,
before he led the horse to fetch grain,
or cart beans, vetch, oats and hay to feed the stock;
scything, threshing and heaving sheaves was hard,

but winter harder, breaking clods, carting dung to lay
on fallow fields, mending frosted tracks, chopping wood.
And the others, were they at the service just now?
The man who sang the bass part, he was the cowherd,
the one who rang the tenor bell led oxen to the plough,
you're sure to find his name; it's my old eyes,
I can't find the place, nor where to lay this posy of mine,
for she loved the meadow knapweed and scent of wayside
eglantine.

Kinship

It is not so much a valley and certainly no ravine,
just a shallow indent in soft-rounded downs
that leads, gently sloping, towards a sea cliff line.
It is not a long walk with hazards or uneven ground,
nor does the weather have unpredictable extremes,
although gusting gales render the edge a place
only for the foolhardy or those with lost dreams.
But it is a warm, welcoming pastorale, laced
with pastel patterns and amalgams of honeyed scents
that cure many sicknesses and restless melancholy.
Its challenges are not as in rugged land that resents
incursions, with a rewarding elation of conquest,
but of submitting to subtlety and tenderness
with the reward of kinship with a welcoming wildness.

One Short Summer

Swallows perch on the north-point vane,
then the east, unsure, to leave or to delay;
go back, go back a guinea fowl encourages
and gulls' swaying echelons show the way.
But thickening grey and gusting wind
urge skittering and chittering time away,
to the reassuring croon of wood doves
professing love of season, place and day.

And Charles and Sarah Russell wish
that summer of 1882 had never flown,
when Jessie May, carried to the meadow,
watched tantalizing globes of thistle down
and blue-green fascinations of damsel flies;
for when October turned to November,
five months and three weeks of sunshine
was all there was to remember.

Shards of Summer

Sunrise shadows defined downland folds,
perfect as wishful thinking, real as rural dreams;
then the disturbance, the air full, vibrant,
in perpetual motion with shards of summer
stirring sun-dust into ephemeral patterns;
one swallow is every swallow, untraceable,
sweep, dart, check and twist over ochreous grass,
in and out of thistledown and teasel heads,
banish a marauding hawk to the seclusion of trees,
hesitate, flutter and dip over a sky-bright ditch,
breaking the spell of an infinite reflection with a kiss.

Take sustenance, for tomorrow, tomorrow,
which of us perceives the import of tomorrow?
Is there an inkling of the journey, anticipation even,
with excitement or anxiety before the communal surge
to leave the tarnished currency of a tired land
for somewhere, some reason the spirit knows.
Prove it otherwise, doubter, naysayer;
feelings are not a privilege given on the sixth day,
for they know, they surely know, but cannot explain,
as we cannot explain love or grief, just feel
in our animal dumbness and weep with happiness or
pain.

Confessions

But then a September storm came,
the worst for thirty years they say,
three days of rain, driven on a gusting gale
that churned a cacophonous whiteness across the bay;
nothing is silent, nothing is at peace.

The incoming tide's steely-surge
turned the river's swollen flow
and swept between hard-tested banks
where gulls picked over flotsam at the eroding edge;
nothing is safe, nothing is secure.

Spray salted and wind-watered eyes,
rain-lashed and wind-trashed senses,
the exhilaration of confrontation,
confirm our place in the confusion and turbulence;
nothing is clear, nothing is understood.

Scraps of blue and fleeting sea-sparkle
seduce swallows' buffeted flight,
low, low over the beach and heading out;
can any desire be so great, such tragedy be right;
nothing is sacred, nothing above fate.

Impotent pleading, howled into the gale,
whipped and scattered with sea-foam
away past the headlands and lost
in pebble rattle and the ocean's grey-misted moan;
nothing is heard, nothing is heeded.

Shriven souls on the shifting beach,
off-balance and battered on the shore,
confessing that, from time to time, we too
have flown headlong to places that promised more;
nothing is reasoned, nothing is rational.

Warts and All

Portraits should be honest.

It is difficult to be otherwise when low-lit,
grey dampness leaches out colour,
shortens horizons and depresses the spirit;
and November is still a week away.
It becomes impossible to turn a blind eye
to unkempt buildings, leaning fences unfixed
and creaking, months after the last high wind.

Things were not always like this.

Carelessly thrown bottles, wrappers and cans
exposed by the die-back of summer's masking
or shifted into decaying rubbish jams.
And there is worse.
Dog latrines and drunken-vomit stains
that hazard pavements and green ways to the sea.

Eyes on the ground to avoid unsavoury remains.

Perhaps storms will wash them away?
Well some of them, for a short time;
cloud breaks may brighten autumn crocus flowers,
salve swallows trapped by sleety wind,
refocus jaundiced eyes and challenge the power
of those unmoved by detritus, dereliction and despair,
not for the need of money, just the currency of care.

Dream on, dream on, dream on.

Lapis Philosophorum

Things that are most sought after
are often stumbled on, rather than found
by diligent searching, and last Sunday,
without premeditation or expectation,
I fulfilled a dream that has engaged humanity
ever since thinkers first thought and seekers sought.

Not just a dream, but the Great Work
of finding the Philosopher's Stone.
Alchemists desired it to turn base metals
into gold and silver, pebbles to jewels,
or, as the basis of all matter and living creatures,
an elixir to rejuvenate or give immortality.

Others were less literal, seeking not an object,
powder or potion, but God-given wisdom
that gave a grasp of the meaning of life;
an amalgam of science, mysticism, philosophy
and spirituality concocted in the mind's crucible;
and I am prepared to tell you how I found it.

It started with a short walk, slip-sliding
down the track, glossy with wet chalk sheen,
then through the gate, no protecting spirits,
just algal slime and water dripping branches,
to where the view opened like a picture book
over the scarp on High and Over hill.

It was a dreary, diminished landscape,
the steep east-facing slope deep in shadow,
the wind raw, the valley below bleak,
with a silt-soiled river and flooded meadows
pewter-grey, reflecting nothing, the woods
on far slopes an indefinable monochrome.

A hawk and a falcon rose from the shadows
and in sweeping gyres challenged for the right
to the sky; as they rose above the ridge
the clouds broke, turning their feathers to gold,
distant downs became a cloth of gold
and the river a flow of diamond glistening.

Four crows joined the hawk and falcon
and reformed as silvered crosses,
on leafless twigs, drops of the morning's rain
were strings of rubies, amethysts and emeralds,
and on the sodden turf, eyes awash with the wind,
I was young again.

BIBLIOGRAPHY

CASTLEDEN, Rodney. The Wilmington Giant. Blatchington Press 2012

COCKER, Mark. Birds Britannica. Chatto and Windus 2005

GRIGSON, Geoffrey. The Englishman's Flora. Paladin 1975

MARREN, Peter. Bugs Britannica. Chatto and Windus 2010

MABEY, Richard. Flora Britannica. Sinclair-Stevenson 1996

MACDERMOTT, Rev. K.H. The Church Gallery Minstrels of Old Sussex. Country Books 2006

WILKINSON, Edwin. Downland Heritage. S.B. Publications 2008

WOODS, Rollo G. Good Singing Still. West Gallery Music Association 1995

I am also indebted to information leaflets provided by the churches at Alciston, Friston, Folkington, Jevington, Litlington, Wilmington and East Guldeford.